W9-ALL-109

Ethiopia

by Spencer Brinker

Consultant: Marjorie Faulstich Orellana, PhD
Professor of Urban Schooling
University of California, Los Angeles

BEARPORT
PUBLISHING

New York, New York

MOORESTOWN LIBRARY
111 W. SECOND STREET
MOORESTOWN, NJ 08057-2481
(856) 234-0333
www.moorestown.lib.nj.us

Credits

Cover, © Nick Fox/Shutterstock and © skynesher/iStock; TOC, © Dereje/Shutterstock; 4, © Aleksandra H. Kossowska/Shutterstock; 5L, © Lost Horizon Images/AGE Fotostock; 5R, © Magdalena Paluchowska/Shutterstock; 7, © Grant Rooney Premium/Alamy; 8, © guenterguni/iStock; 8T, © Stefan Auth/imageBROKER/Alamy; 9, © Radek Borovka/Shutterstock; 10T, © Andrew Harrington/NPL/Minden Pictures; 10B, © guenterguni/iStock; 11, © Juan Carlos Muñoz/AGE Fotostock; 12L, © Zoonar/Dereje Belach/AGE Fotostock; 12–13, © Dmitry Chulov/Shutterstock; 14T, © Jon Bower-art and museums/Alamy; 14B, © Chronicle/Alamy; 15, © Anton_Ivanov/Shutterstock; 16, © robertharding/Alamy; 17, © Edwin Remsberg/Alamy; 18, © Bridgeman Images; 19L, © justinfoster/iStock; 19R, © robertharding/Alamy; 20T, © pr2is/Shutterstock; 20B, © bonchan/Shutterstock; 21, © Boaz Rottem/Alamy; 22, © guenterguni/iStock; 23, © Bartosz Hadyniak/iStock; 24, © Anton_Ivanov/Shutterstock; 25T, © dpa picture alliance/Alamy; 25B, © pukach/Shutterstock; 26, © guenterguni/iStock; 27TL, © Anton_Ivanov/Shutterstock; 27BL, © Sarine Arsianian/Shutterstock; 27R, © gomolach/Shutterstock; 28, © Simon Balson/Alamy; 29, © Eric Lafforgue/AGE Fotostock; 30T, © Oleg_Mit/Shutterstock, © Anton_Ivanov/Shutterstock, and © Asafta/Dreamstime; 30B, © Lanmas/Alamy; 31 (T to B), © Dmitry Chulov/Shutterstock, © Nick Fox/Shutterstock, © Kobby Dagan/Shutterstock, © Millenius/Shutterstock, © DavidLovincic/iStock, and © Martin Good/Shutterstock; 32, © Solodov Aleksey/Shutterstock.

Publisher: Kenn Goin
Senior Editor: Joyce Tavolacci
Creative Director: Spencer Brinker
Design: Debrah Kaiser
Photo Researcher: Thomas Persano

Library of Congress Cataloging-in-Publication Data

Names: Brinker, Spencer, author.
Title: Ethiopia / by Spencer Brinker.
Description: New York, New York : Bearport Publishing, [2018] | Series:
   Countries we come from | Includes bibliographical references and index.
Identifiers: LCCN 2017039219 (print) | LCCN 2017039866 (ebook) | ISBN
   9781684025299 (ebook) | ISBN 9781684024711 (library binding)
Subjects: LCSH: Ethiopia—Juvenile literature.
Classification: LCC DT373 (ebook) | LCC DT373 .B686 (print) | DDC 963—dc23
LC record available at https://lccn.loc.gov/2017039219

Copyright © 2018 Bearport Publishing Company, Inc. All rights reserved. No part of this publication may be reproduced in whole or in part, stored in any retrieval system, or transmitted in any form or by any means, electronic, mechanical, photocopying, recording, or otherwise, without written permission from the publisher.

For more information, write to Bearport Publishing Company, Inc., 45 West 21st Street, Suite 3B, New York, New York 10010. Printed in the United States of America.

10 9 8 7 6 5 4 3 2 1

Contents

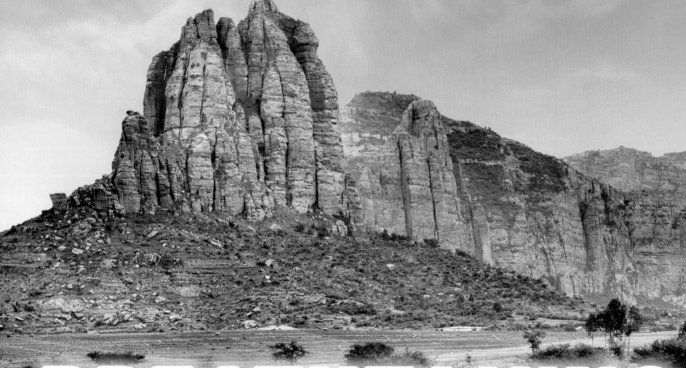

BREATHTAKING

Friendly

Colorful

5

Ethiopia is a large country in Africa.

It's about as big as Texas and California put together!

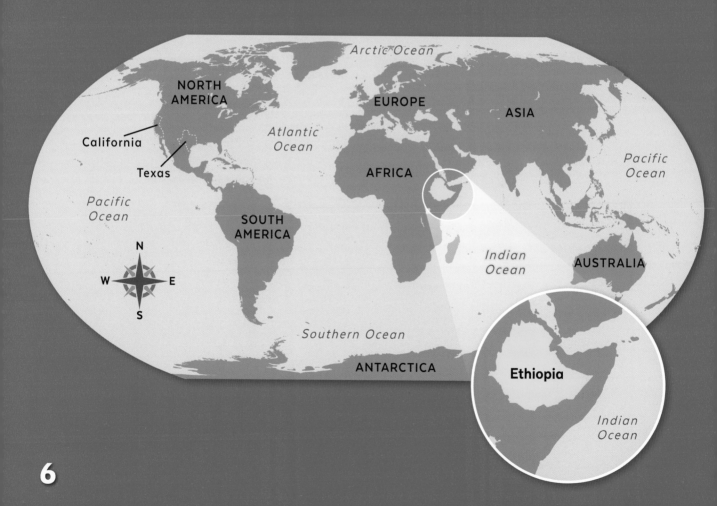

More than 100 million people live in Ethiopia.

Ethiopia has many different types of land.

There are mountains, deserts, and forests.

forest

desert

8

Ethiopia's Great Rift Valley has huge, dry **plateaus**.

plateau

A rift is a large crack or split in the earth.

Amazing animals live in Ethiopia.

Rare Ethiopian wolves roam the mountains.

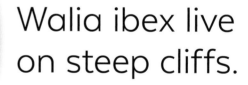

Walia ibex live on steep cliffs.

Furry geladas munch on the mountain grass.

A gelada is a type of monkey. Geladas have a patch of bright red skin on their chests.

Addis Ababa is the **capital** of Ethiopia.

It's also the country's largest city.

More than three million people live there!

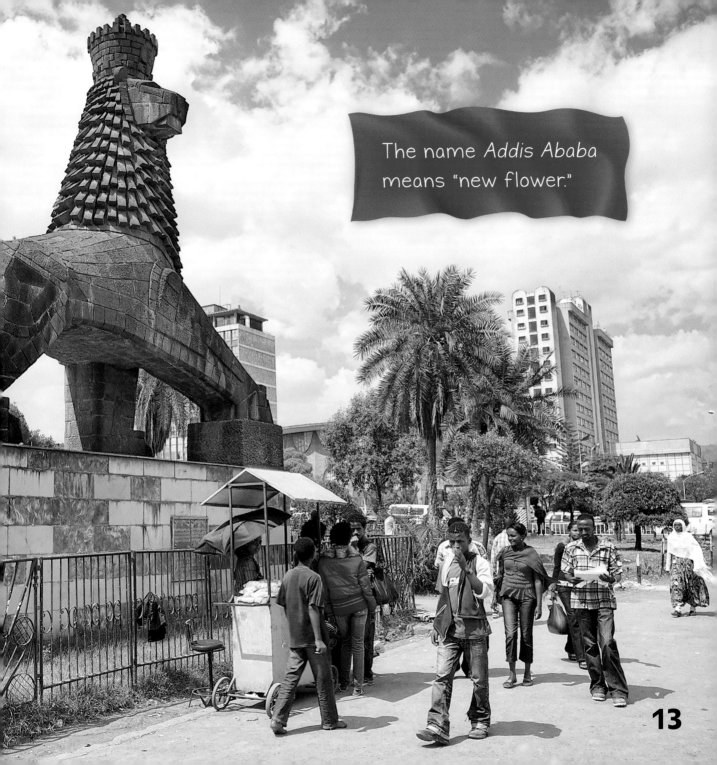

The name *Addis Ababa* means "new flower."

Ethiopia has worked hard for its freedom.

Twice the country has fought wars to keep its **independence**.

In 1916, a woman named Zewditu became Ethiopia's ruler. She was the country's first woman leader in hundreds of years.

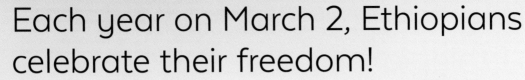

Each year on March 2, Ethiopians celebrate their freedom!

15

Many languages are spoken in Ethiopia.

Amharic is the most common.

This is how you say *hello* to friends in Amharic:

Selam
(sa-LAM)

This is how you say *hello*
to teachers and other adults:

Tena yistilign
(ten-AH YIS-til-in)

Oromo is another language
spoken in Ethiopia.

17

Several of Ethiopia's languages use the Ge'ez alphabet.

It's one of the oldest alphabets still in use!

Ge'ez letters can be found on many **ancient** artifacts.

old stone carving

Modern signs in Ethiopia are also written in Ge'ez.

19

Hungry? Ethiopian food is delicious!

Meat stews called *wat* are served with vegetables.

The food is arranged on a flat, spongy bread called *injera*.

injera

wat

Ethiopians use injera to scoop up their food. Yum!

21

After a big meal, it's time for a coffee **ceremony**.

Coffee beans are roasted, ground, and boiled in front of guests.

roasting coffee beans

The oldest person gets the first cup!

Salt is sometimes added to Ethiopian coffee instead of sugar!

23

Many Ethiopians are farmers.

They grow coffee, corn, and sugarcane.

Ethiopian coffee is famous around the world!

Some Ethiopian farmers grow colorful flowers.

25

What time is it?

In Ethiopia, time is based on when the sun rises and sets.

There are 12 hours of daytime, and 12 hours of nighttime!

Ethiopian time is organized differently than standard time. For example, our 7:00 A.M. is called 1:00 in the day in Ethiopia.

Standard Time	Ethiopian Time
7:00 A.M.	1:00 in the day
12:00 P.M.	6:00 in the day
7:00 P.M.	1:00 at night
12:00 A.M.	6:00 at night

What sport is popular in Ethiopia?

Running!

Ethiopian runners are known for their speed and **stamina**.

Many have won Olympic gold medals!

Soccer is also
a popular sport.

29

Fast Facts

Capital city: Addis Ababa

Population of Ethiopia: More than 100 million

Main languages: Amharic, Oromo, Somali, and Tigrinya

Money: Birr

Major religions: Christianity and Islam

Neighboring countries: Eritrea, Sudan, Kenya, Somalia, and Djibouti

Cool Fact: The remains of an early human were discovered in Ethiopia in 1974. The famous bones are about 3.2 million years old!

ancient (AYN-shunt) from a long time ago

capital (KAP-uh-tuhl) a city where a country's government is based

ceremony (SER-uh-moh-nee) an event that marks a special occasion

independence (in-duh-PEN-duhnss) the state of being free from control by others

plateaus (pla-TOHS) areas of high, flat land

stamina (STAM-uh-nuh) the strength and energy to do something over a long period of time

Index

Read More

Heinrichs, Ann. *Ethiopia (Enchantment of the World).* New York: Scholastic (2005).

Pohl, Kathleen. *Looking at Ethiopia (Looking at Countries).* New York: Gareth Stevens (2008).

Learn More Online

To learn more about Ethiopia, visit
www.bearportpublishing.com/CountriesWeComeFrom

About the Author

Spencer Brinker lives and works in New York City. He loves Ethiopian food and hopes to visit the beautiful country one day.